POLAND

RICHARD WORTH

POLAND

THE THREAT TO NATIONAL RENEWAL

A GROLIER COMPANY

FRANKLIN WATTS

New York | London | Sydney | Toronto | 1982

AN IMPACT BOOK

Photographs courtesy of United Press International Photo

Map courtesy of Vantage Art, Inc.

Library of Congress Cataloging in Publication Data

Worth, Richard
Poland, the threat to national renewal.

(An Impact book)
Bibliography: p.
Includes index.
Summary: Discusses the history of Poland,
focusing on the rise of Communism;
the formation of Solidarity, a collection
of local unions; and the response of
the Soviets and the Communist leaders
in Warsaw to Solidarity.
1. Poland—History—1945- —Juvenile literature.
2. NSZZ "Solidarność" (Labor organization)
—Juvenile literature.   [1. Poland—History.
2. Solidarity (Polish labor organization)
3. Labor unions] I. Title.
DK4433.W67   943.8   82-2558
ISBN 0-531-04424-6   AACR2

CONTENTS

POLAND

INTRODUCTION

In August 1980 Polish shipyard workers at the Lenin shipyard in the Baltic port city of Gdansk stopped work, closed the gates to the shipyard, and went on strike. The workers were protesting recent food shortages and what they felt was an unreasonable increase in meat prices by the Communist government. Such increases had occurred on a few occasions in the past. Each time workers in Poland had protested, and each time the government had retreated.

A few hours after the strike had started, a thirty-seven-year-old unemployed electrician with a drooping mustache climbed over the walls of the shipyard. Soon he was being hailed as the strike leader. The man was known to the other workers. In fact he had been employed at the shipyard until he was fired for being a "political troublemaker." Subsequently, he had gained quite a reputation as a champion of workers' rights against a Communist regime which refused to recognize them.

This man's name was Lech Walesa.

As the strikers watched and waited for the government to do something, their movement gained momentum. Along the Baltic and in other parts of Poland, 270,000 workers walked off their jobs in a show of support. Poland's powerful Catholic church also gave its backing to the strikers as Catholic priests came to the shipyard to hear confessions and say masses.

Inside the shipyard the workers unfurled banners which read: "No meat, no bread, no butter. All we have to eat are the words of Lenin." The workers not only wanted an end to Poland's food problems, they also wanted greater freedom under the Communist government. Soon they had drawn up a list of demands which included the right to form independent trade unions—something unheard of in a Communist bloc country, where the Communists claim to represent the workers.

But most Poles have never really accepted Communism. Instead they have clung tenaciously to a strong spirit of nationalism that is many centuries old. The strikers adopted as their emblem the Polish national flag, and throughout the strike they continued to sing the words of Poland's national anthem: "Poland has not yet perished."

After seventeen days of strikes which threatened further damage to Poland's already shaky economy, the Communist government capitulated and agreed to the workers' demands. The agreement was signed by a top Communist official and strike leader Lech Walesa, who used a long red and white pen which had been given to him by Poland's own, Pope John Paul II, during a visit to the country a year earlier.

Perhaps it was a fitting conclusion to a historic agreement that sought to change Poland so decisively. For it represented a victory for the forces of Polish nationalism, freedom and Catholicism—three dominant forces that have sustained Poland throughout its long and difficult past.

CHAPTER 1 • POLISH BEGINNINGS

Poland—*Polska* in the Polish language—means "the land of the plain." Poland is located on the flat plains of central Europe—a geography which has left the country unprotected, especially from its eastern and western neighbors. On the east, Poland is bordered by Russia; on the west by what is now East Germany. To the north, Poland lies on the Baltic Sea, and in the south, mountain ranges separate the country from Czechoslovakia. Warsaw became the capital of Poland in the sixteenth century after a fire burned the former capital, Krakow, located farther south. Both cities lie on the long Vistula River, which rises in the mountains bordering Czechoslovakia and empties into the Baltic Sea near the large port city of Gdansk.

The Polish state arose along the valleys of the Vistula and other rivers during the Middle Ages. In 966, Duke Mieszko I proclaimed himself ruler of some of the tribes in the area. In the same year he became a Christian. From these modest beginnings the Catholic church rose to become one of the most powerful institutions in Poland, a position it still holds today. Over the next few centuries Polish fortunes rose and fell as the Poles battled over land with their neighbors, the Germans. This began a pattern that would be part of Polish history into modern times.

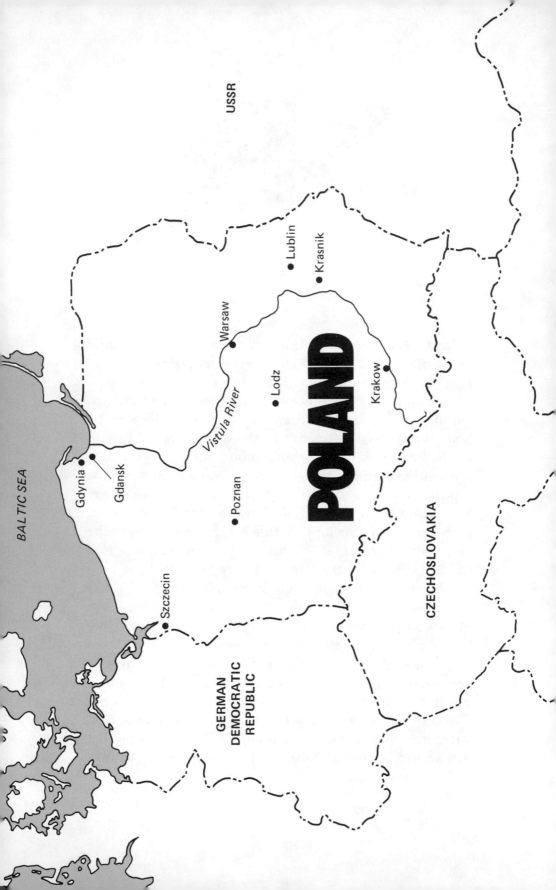

During the fourteenth century, the Polish empire expanded until it stretched from the Baltic to the Black Sea. In the years that followed, especially during the sixteenth century, Poland would enjoy a golden age in the arts, architecture, and the sciences. One of the most famous men of this period was Nicholas Copernicus, a Polish astronomer and the first European to write that the planets in our solar system revolve around the sun.

THE DECLINE OF POLAND
While Poland enjoyed the cultural Renaissance, a political struggle was occurring between the kings and the landed nobility, who wanted to limit the monarch's power. Finally, during the sixteenth century, and afterward, the nobles succeeded in transferring much of this power to the Sejm, or parliament, which was controlled by the nobility and the Catholic clergy. Unfortunately the Sejm was unable to defend Poland against its neighbors. During the seventeenth and eighteenth centuries, hostile armies overran Poland and laid waste its farms and cities.

The empires of Russia, Prussia, and Austria took advantage of Poland's weakness and partitioned, or divided, the country three times in the latter part of the eighteenth century. In response to the second partition General Tadeusz Kosciuszko, a hero of the American Revolution who had returned to his native Poland, led a revolt among the Polish people. The revolt was crushed with great cruelty by Russia and Prussia. To prevent a further outbreak, they joined with Austria to partition Poland for the third time in 1795. The entire country was gobbled up, and the Kingdom of Poland vanished from the map of Europe.

The Poles never forgot Kosciuszko's revolt. Its proud memory lived on and came to symbolize the spirit of romantic heroism and recklessness which is such an important part of the Polish character. As one Pole explained: "The perfect way of death for a Pole is to die on his horse while fording a river under a hail of enemy bullets."

The spirit of Polish nationalism and independence lived on, too. Throughout the nineteenth century, the Polish people revolted again and again. In 1830 the revolt lasted ten months, but the Polish army was finally defeated by the Russians who entered Warsaw as conquerors. In 1863 following another uprising, Russia and Prussia clamped down on Polish society attempting ruthlessly to stamp out the spirit of Polish nationalism. As a result of these experiences, the Poles developed a special hatred for their two powerful neighbors to the east and west.

A NEW POLISH STATE
The outbreak of World War I in 1914 found Poland in an unusual situation. The three empires which had been allied against it now fought on opposite sides. Germany and Austria-Hungary were members of the Central Powers, while Russia had joined Britain and France. Polish political leaders believed that if they backed the winning side they might be rewarded, and Poland would be granted its independence. The only question was which side to back. One group supported Russia. Another supported the Central Powers.

The leader of the second group was Jozef Pilsudski. He was a former medical student who had become a revolutionary. In 1887 Pilsudski had been exiled from Poland for attempting to assassinate the Russian czar. After the charges were proved false, Pilsudski returned to Poland and joined the Polish Socialist party in 1894. The Socialists believed in the revolution of the masses against social injustice and in the establishment of an independent Polish state.

During the early part of World War I, Pilsudski led his Polish Legion against the Russians. Russia suffered numerous defeats and by 1916 lay exhausted at the hands of the Central Powers. At this point, Pilsudski hoped the victors would grant Poland its independence. But he was sorely disappointed, for the leaders of the Central Powers announced that they would continue to control Poland's destiny. Thereafter, Pilsudski switched loyalties and threw his vigorous support to the Allied Powers.

Polish independence was proclaimed as one of the goals of the Allies. In his famous peace program called the Fourteen Points, President Woodrow Wilson advocated the following:

> *An independent Polish state should be erected which would include the territories inhabited by indisputably Polish population, which would be assured a free and secure access to the sea, and whose political and economic independence and territorial integrity should be guaranteed by international covenant.*

In November 1918, with the Allies finally victorious, the Poles established an independent republic. Pilsudski, who had become a hero during the war for his efforts to achieve Polish sovereignty, became the first head of state. For a brief period in the 1920s Poland tried democracy. But Pilsudski became so displeased with the democratic form of government that he abandoned it and ruled as a virtual dictator until his death in 1936.

Pilsudski and his successors hoped to maintain Poland's independence by steering a middle course between Russia and Germany. Russia had become a Communist state following the overthrow of the czar in 1917. Pilsudski had never regarded the Russians as friends, and the Communists posed just as great a threat as the czars. In 1919 Poland and Russia went to war. The Soviet forces invaded Poland, but Pilsudski defeated them outside Warsaw. Afterward the Poles and the Russians established peaceful relations. But a small Communist party which opposed the government later sprung up inside Poland.

Germany, although defeated in World War I, began to rise again in the 1930s under Nazi leader Adolf Hitler. The Nazis rebuilt the German war machine and began menacing the states that bordered Germany. In 1938 Hitler annexed Austria. The following year he occupied Czechoslovakia. He also threatened to march into Poland. But Germany and Russia still remained enemies. In fact, the forces of Nazism and Communism had vowed to destroy each other. As long as this situation continued and the Poles did not antagonize Russia, they might be safe. Hitler did not dare attack Poland while he feared Russia might march against him.

But on August 23, 1939, Russia and Germany stunned the world. They signed a nonaggression treaty, agreeing not to make war on each other. The treaty also included plans for a partition of Poland. On September 1, the German armies began World War II by invading Poland. Later that month Russia invaded from the east. By the end of September the Polish state had ceased to exist. Poland had been gobbled up by its powerful neighbors, just like so many times in the past.

POLAND DURING THE WAR

World War II is one of the darkest pages in Polish history. Well over six million Poles died during the war. Most of them did not die in battle. In the Russian sector, Poles were deported to the Soviet Union, and many were murdered. At the Katyn Forest, near Smolensk in central Russia, thousands of captured Polish officers were massacred and buried in a mass grave.

Nazi atrocities were even worse. One Pole explained that in his country the "Germans have shown what Europe would look like after a Nazi victory: Nowhere has

the Nazi terror reached such monstrous proportions."
Many Poles were shipped off to Germany to work in labor
camps producing material for the Nazi war effort. Others,
especially Jews, were transported to concentration camps
such as Majdanek, Treblinka, and Auschwitz, which the
Germans established in Poland. In these camps, millions
were slaughtered.

The spirit of Polish nationalism did not die during
these dark days. Poles formed resistance groups just as
they had during the years of Russian and German occupation in the nineteenth century. Polish guerrillas cut rail-
road and communication lines and murdered German
officers. The pre-war Polish government remained alive,
too. After fleeing Poland, they established a "government
in exile" in London from which they urged their people
to continue fighting.

Hitler's alliance with Russia had been designed as
only a short-term measure to protect his eastern flank
while he conquered Western Europe. By 1941 this task
was almost complete, and he turned his attention east-
ward. On June 22, the Nazi dictator invaded Russia. Hitler's invasion seemed to catch Soviet leader Joseph Stalin
by surprise. The Russian armies retreated before the power of the German war machine which rolled on toward
Moscow and Leningrad. It was not until the Nazis were
within a few miles of Moscow that the Russian soldiers
dug in and stopped them. In the meantime, Leningrad
held out against the Nazis and braced for a long and terrible siege.

In 1942 the Russian armed forces bounced back. At
Stalingrad they surrounded and destroyed part of the
German army. Soon they began driving the Nazis back
across eastern Europe. As the Germans retreated the Polish government in London gained hope. Polish leaders
felt their country might recapture its independence, as it

had after World War I. They spoke to the allied leaders—President Franklin D. Roosevelt and British Prime Minister Winston Churchill—and tried to persuade them to re-establish a free Poland. But Stalin had different ideas.

In 1942 the Russians established a new Communist party for Poland called the Polish Workers' Party (PPR). It included the survivors of the small Communist party established in Poland between the wars as well as some new members. In 1944, as the Red Army swept the Nazis out of Poland, the leaders of the PPR were transported to Lublin, a Polish city. They and other Communist supporters established a new provisional government called the Lublin Committee. This was the government that Stalin recognized rather than the Polish government in exile in London. Although Churchill and Roosevelt might disagree with Stalin, they urgently needed his support to defeat Germany, so they went along with him.

At first the Communist government in Poland was very weak. But during the days that followed Stalin made sure that its position improved. In August 1944, as Soviet forces advanced on Warsaw, Polish resistance groups rose up against the Nazis. The Poles expected help from the Russians, but Stalin ordered his soldiers to stand by and do nothing. The Nazis crushed the revolt and killed about 200,000 Polish patriots. The significance of this event was explained by a member of the Lublin Committee:

> Had [the resistance groups] succeeded in liberating Warsaw, they would have been the heroes of Poland and would have formed the nucleus of the government within Poland. It would have been most difficult under such circumstances for the Soviet government to maintain in power the Lublin Committee . . .

As the Nazis retreated to Berlin, the allied leaders met in February 1945 at Yalta in the former summer palace of the

Russian czars. At the Yalta Conference, Roosevelt, Churchill, and Stalin reached many agreements that would affect world affairs after the war had ended. In one of these agreements, the allied leaders recognized the Lublin Committee as the government of Poland. The government was to be "reorganized on a broader democratic basis, with universal suffrage and secret ballot." All "democratic and anti-Nazi parties" were eligible to participate.

Stalin began to undermine this agreement immediately. An expert on Poland, M.K. Dziewanowski, writes in *Poland in the 20th Century* that in March sixteen members of the Polish resistance were invited to take part in "friendly" talks which would help prevent any conflict between their own soldiers and the Soviet army. The resistance leaders disappeared and were taken to Moscow where the Russians charged them with sabotage. This eliminated some of the most effective opposition leaders to the Communist-controlled Lublin Committee.

THE TWILIGHT OF POLAND

At the end of World War II the Poles were facing the loss of their independence once again. The years of freedom had been brief, barely more than two decades in the modern era.

While Stalin might try to stamp out Polish independence, he could not destroy the Polish spirit. The strong sense of Polish nationalism remained. The Poles had not forgotten their heroes, Kosciuszko and Pilsudski. The Catholic church remained a strong rallying point for the Polish people; during the war, Catholic clergy had performed many acts of great courage and daring. Poles were also bound together by their long-standing hatred of the Russians. They regarded everything Russian as inferior because it came from the east. The Poles had always faced westward and identified with Western culture.

As evidence of the endurance of this national spirit, Polish historians have often noted an interesting pattern in their country's past. When Poland is occupied by a foreign power, its people become submissive and politically inactive, almost as if they are in a state of sleep. Then the Poles suddenly awaken, rise up, and attempt to throw off the invader.

CHAPTER II
COMMUNISM TRIUMPHANT

In the years just following the end of World War II, 1945–1948, Stalin established a Russian empire in eastern Europe which included the countries of East Germany, Hungary, Rumania, Bulgaria, Czechoslovakia, and Poland. In each of these countries, the Soviet dictator insured the victory of Communism by using the power of the Red Army as well as political intrigue and terror.[1]

There are many reasons why Stalin was so ruthlessly intent on establishing an empire in eastern Europe. First, according to experts in Soviet affairs, he wanted to prevent the region from falling into the hands of a country hostile to Russia. Hitler had used the years before World War II and the period of the Russo-German alliance to occupy brutally most of eastern Europe. Then he used the region as a springboard for his lightning invasion of Russia which took Stalin so completely by surprise. Stalin wanted to avoid a similar invasion in the future, and he believed that the countries of eastern Europe would serve

[1] In Albania, the Communists gained control without the help of Russian power. Albania has moved in and out of the Soviet empire, always pursuing an isolated and somewhat independent course.

as a strong defensive barrier to prevent another sneak attack.

A second reason for Stalin's desire to control eastern Europe was to use the area's resources to help rebuild the Soviet economy. World War II had taken an enormous toll on the resources of the Soviet Union. Millions of Russian people had lost their lives, and many industries had been completely destroyed during the Nazi invasions. Following the war, Red Army troops looted the occupied eastern countries of heavy machinery and other items that could be used to refit Russian factories. Stalin also intended to force these countries to sell their raw materials and finished products to the Soviet Union at cheap prices.

Finally, Stalin wanted eastern Europe as a springboard from which he could launch an offensive against the West. This could be a military or a political attack designed to undermine the western governments and to overthrow their leaders. Alternatively, eastern European countries could become a Communist showcase demonstrating the success of Communism and influencing Western political leaders to adopt it.

COMMUNISM IN POLAND

In Poland the Communists faced a far more difficult task in taking control of the government than they did in some other eastern countries. As M.K. Dziewanowski points out, Poland had a very strong Catholic church. And the church actively opposed Communism. The country was also essentially agricultural with a relatively small working class which the Communists traditionally depended upon for support. Finally, there was the overwhelming Polish hatred of anything Russian—a hatred which had only been increased by the massacre at Katyn Forest and by other Russian atrocities.

But the Communists in Poland did possess important advantages. They stood united, while the opposition was divided. They also had the backing of the mighty Red Army. The Communists used these advantages skillfully to make alliances with other political groups who believed that the future of Poland lay in a coalition government which included Communists as well as non-Communists.

To gather further support among the Polish people, the Communists gave the Catholic church more freedom than it was permitted in other eastern countries. Poles were allowed to listen to foreign radio broadcasts—and farmers were assured that their land would not be taken and turned into collectives, the large government-owned farms which existed in Russia.

In addition to trying to win the hearts of the Polish people, the Communist party turned its attention to rebuilding the Polish economy. From 1945–1948, many industries were nationalized, taken over and run by the government. Industrial output expanded enormously, although the emphasis was not on consumer items, but on so-called heavy industry such as steel production. Near the city of Krakow, the Communists constructed the Lenin Steel Works and built a new town, Nowa Huta, to house the workers. Throughout this period, many Poles left the farms to take jobs in industry. The Communists encouraged this movement because it meant more supporters for their party.

While the Communists tightened their grip on Poland's economy, they also sought to increase their political power. In January 1947 democratic elections were scheduled to be held, according to agreements reached at Yalta. The Communists still faced political opposition, so before the election they carried on a vicious campaign which included mass arrests of their opponents, raids on their headquarters, and the removal of their opponents' names from the ballot. When the election results were announced, the Communists had won an overwhelming victory. Their control of Poland now seemed complete.

COMMUNIST OPPRESSION INCREASES

Until the elections of 1947, Poles still enjoyed more freedom than the people of other Communist countries. After these elections Polish freedom became a thing of the past. Since the Polish Communists had consolidated their power, they no longer needed to win the support of opposition groups.

Life inside Poland was also being directly influenced by events outside the country. Relations between the Soviet Union and the Western allies were growing steadily worse. Friction had already developed over the so-called democratic elections in Poland. At the same time, Communist-led guerrilla bands were threatening the governments of Greece and Turkey. In the face of these guerrilla attacks, President Truman decided the time had come for the United States to take action. In 1947 the President announced his Truman Doctrine:

> *I believe that it must be the policy of the United States to support free peoples who are resisting attempted subjugation by armed minorities or by outside pressures. I believe that we must assist free peoples to work out their own destinies in their own way.*

Truman then asked Congress for $400 million in aid to help Greece and Turkey.

In that same year the United States proposed the Marshall Plan, named after Secretary of State George C. Marshall. The program was designed to assist the economic recovery of Europe, which lay devastated after World War II. Another major purpose of the plan was to strengthen the nations of western Europe against Communism.

Western Europe also established military alliances aimed at combating Communism. In 1948 Great Britain, France, Luxembourg, Belgium, and the Netherlands signed the Treaty of Brussels. The following year this became the North Atlantic Treaty Organization (NATO), which included the United States as well as other Western countries.

As Stalin looked out from Moscow, the West must have seemed like an armed camp arrayed against him. There were rumblings within eastern Europe, too. A dispute broke out between Stalin and Marshal Tito, the Communist dictator of Yugoslavia. Most of the Yugoslav Communists supported Tito, and in 1948 he finally broke with Stalin and began to pursue a course independent of the Soviet Union.

In response to all these international developments Stalin grew extremely concerned about the security of the Soviet empire, and he tightened his control over the Communist satellite countries in eastern Europe. Within Poland, any Communists who did not agree with Stalin were purged immediately. One of these was Wladyslaw Gomulka, secretary-general of the Communist party.[1] Although he accepted the presence of the Soviet Union in eastern Europe, Gomulka did not believe that each of the satellite countries should adopt a carbon copy of Russian Communism. He believed in the "Polish path to socialism," a brand of Communism which allowed the Poles some independence within the Soviet orbit. Stalin, however, was not about to allow anything that smacked of Titoism, especially in one of the leaders of the Polish Communist party. Gomulka lost his position in 1948 and was later arrested.

---

[1] In 1948 the Communist and Socialist parties merged to become the Polish United Workers' Party (PZPR). In this book, however, it will be referred to simply as the Communist party.

Stalin's policies affected every facet of Polish life. M.K. Dziewanowski describes the years between 1948 and 1953 as a period of "increasing terror" which "created an atmosphere of acute tension, alienation and hopelessness." Many died in the terror.

Many people looked to the Catholic church for support and hope during these dark days. But even the church was not spared from Stalin's wrath. Church property was seized, and Catholic clerics were thrown into prison. The state-controlled press led a violent attack on Stefan Cardinal Wyszynski, the leader of Poland's Catholics, who was finally arrested in 1953.

Stalin tried to force everyone to do his will. Since he had reason to suspect the loyalty of Polish army leaders, he removed them and appointed Russians to take their places. Polish peasants suffered, too. Many lost their land and were forced onto huge collectives, the state-owned farms.

In 1950 the Korean War broke out. Stalin supplied the North Koreans in their conflict against South Korea, which was supported by the United States and its allies. Stalin expected every country in the eastern bloc to assist the Soviets in the war effort. As a result, the Polish Communists stepped up their efforts to expand Poland's industry, ruthlessly driving the workers to increase their output.

By 1953 Poland appeared to be completely under the control of Moscow. On the surface, at least, Stalin had succeeded. But as the Polish Communists tried to carry out his directives, they were losing the support of the Polish people. This might cause problems in the future.

POLAND AFTER STALIN
In 1953 Stalin died. Gradually conditions within his empire began to change. The new Soviet leadership, headed by Nikita Khrushchev, quietly began relaxing

Stalin's reign of terror. Then at the Twentieth Congress of the Soviet Communist Party, Khrushchev went so far as to openly denounce Stalin for his mistakes.

The attack on Stalin had an immediate effect inside Poland. It gave the signal to all the groups that had been suppressed during the Stalinist reign of terror to begin loudly criticizing the Polish Communist regime. Church leaders, peasants, workers, and intellectuals demanded greater freedom. They also wanted an improvement in the standard of living. Although the Communists had succeeded in improving Polish industry, they had neglected to provide the country with enough food.

Polish Communist leaders realized that in order to regain the support of the Polish people they would have to grant some of their demands. A few pro-Stalinists, widely hated in the country, were dismissed from their posts in the government. The Communist leaders also sought the advice of former Secretary-General Wladyslaw Gomulka. During his arrest, Gomulka had become a hero to the Polish people because of his independent stand against Stalin. The Communists had released Gomulka, and now they sought to use his popularity to curry favor among the masses.

But the Poles wanted far more.

On June 28, 1956, fifty thousand Polish workers went on strike and began demonstrating in the city of Poznan, chanting "bread and freedom"; the strikers demanded better living conditions and more independence from Soviet control. The government called out the army and brutally put down the strike, killing some of the workers and wounding many others.

The Poznan revolt had demonstrated the strong opposition to Communism inside Poland and touched off an intense debate within the upper ranks of the Communist party. The conservatives, or hard-liners, wanted to clamp down on Polish society and ignore demands for greater freedom. But more liberal members of the party believed that additional reforms were necessary. They realized that a broad gulf existed between the party and the people, and unless this gulf was closed the Communists might be overthrown. Both factions were agreed on this: there was only one man who could save the situation—Gomulka. The hard-liners wanted to give Gomulka only a secondary position in the party where they could control him. However, the liberals were intent on making Gomulka party leader so he could institute necessary reforms and regain support for the Communist party.

While the return of Gomulka might be greeted with enthusiasm among many Communists and non-Communists in Poland, the Soviet leaders still opposed him. Although Khrushchev might criticize many of Stalin's methods, he still agreed with the basic policy of preserving a secure Russian empire in eastern Europe. In the past, men like Gomulka had posed a threat to this empire with their belief in the "Polish path to socialism." And there was no reason to think that Gomulka's views had changed during the period of his confinement.

On October 19, 1956, the Central Committee of the Polish Communist party met in Warsaw. The meeting was attended by Gomulka. Although the hard-liners still wanted to keep him under their control, there was wide popular support for Gomulka in Warsaw and in other parts of the country. It was therefore expected that he would be appointed first-secretary, leader of the party.

Suddenly, a Russian delegation led by Khrushchev flew into Warsaw and interrupted the meeting of the Central Committee. They had come to stop Gomulka's appointment. Soviet troops stationed in Poland began to advance toward the capital. To counter this threat Polish armed forces loyal to Gomulka were put on alert in Warsaw. A bloody conflict might break out at any moment.

In the meantime Khrushchev and his associates met in a stormy session with Gomulka and the other Polish Communist leaders. There is no report of the exact words spoken by the Russian leader or the Polish party officials. But after the meeting ended, Khrushchev returned to Moscow. Gomulka returned to the meeting of the Central Committee of the Polish Communist party and was selected first-secretary.

THE POLISH OCTOBER

Poland's victory over the Soviets was very significant. It demonstrated that the spirit of Polish nationalism and independence remained alive.

Despite Stalin's efforts to impose his will on the Polish people, they had never surrendered. The Catholic church had remained a powerful institution, providing hope and inspiration for millions of Polish Catholics. Although Stalin had attempted to force Polish farmers onto collectives, only a small percentage of the land ever became state-owned, far less than in any other Soviet satellite. In the other eastern bloc countries, Communists who disagreed with Stalin usually had been killed. But in Poland some men like Gomulka had survived to return to power after the death of the Soviet dictator.

Gomulka was fifty-one when he became first-secretary. He had joined the small Communist party of Poland in 1926 and had participated in workers' strikes during the 1930s. In World War II Gomulka organized the Communist underground movement and in 1943 became secretary-general of the new Polish Workers' Party. He was later elected to the Politburo, the party's ruling body, and held a prominent position of leadership in the party until he was dismissed by Stalin and finally arrested.

In his stormy meeting with Khrushchev, Gomulka showed that he could stand up to the Russians and force them to back down. Of course, Gomulka could never have taken such a strong position had he not received the full support of the Polish Communist party. Even the hard-liners recognized that he alone could lead the country. The party leaders had thus demonstrated that they could control the crisis in Poland, and that they had a man in Gomulka who could take charge and restore order. Presented with this situation, Khrushchev decided to leave Poland in the hands of the Polish Communists.

Gomulka wisely did not try to push the Russians too far or demand too much independence for Poland. In November he flew to Moscow where he swore continued allegiance to the Warsaw Pact. This is a military alliance established by the Soviet Union in 1955 which includes all the eastern satellite countries.

Gomulka fully realized the danger in Poland's position. At any time during the October crisis Soviet troops could have marched on Warsaw. The Poles probably would have fought, but in the end they would have been defeated. As one Soviet leader remarked: "We could have crushed them like flies."

A COLD WIND IN HUNGARY

The "Polish October" seems remarkable, especially when it is compared with events occurring at the same time in Hungary. Following the death of Stalin and the attacks on his policies by Soviet leaders, unrest had arisen in Hungary just as it had in Poland. In October 1956 the Hungarians heard about the success of their neighbors in Poland. They now hoped for a similar victory themselves. Hungarian leaders drew up a list of proposals which called for, among other things, change in the Hungarian Communist leadership. However, the more radical student groups went further, demanding free elections and major improvements in the economy.

On October 23, a mass demonstration was held in Budapest, the Hungarian capital, in support of the Poles. The crowds of people grew so large and unruly that the government could not control them. Finally the Hungarian people forced a change in the leadership of the ruling Communist party, just as the Poles had only a few days earlier.

But the new Hungarian leaders were unable to take charge. Demonstrations continued and spread to other parts of the country. The people demanded greater freedom and an end to any Soviet control. In an effort to gain support among the population, Communist leaders agreed to allow new political parties which could run against the Communists in elections. The leaders also declared that Hungary would withdraw from the Warsaw Pact.

At this point the Soviet Union took decisive action. On November 4, Soviet troops staged massive attacks on Budapest and other Hungarian cities. Soviet forces quickly crushed the badly outnumbered Hungarian resistance. The new Communist leaders were removed and later executed by the Soviets, who replaced them with men loyal to Moscow.

Why had the Soviet armies attacked in Hungary and not in Poland? The situation in Hungary had slipped beyond the control of the Communist party there. In the view of the Soviets, the Hungarian Communists had also gone much too far in allowing the formation of opposition political parties and taking Hungary out of the Warsaw Pact. Moscow could not permit this kind of independence which might spread to other eastern bloc countries. Events in Hungary were watched carefully by the Communist leaders in Warsaw. They would remember the "Hungarian November," and it would directly influence their policies in the months and years ahead.

CHAPTER III THE GOMULKA YEARS

In a speech as new first-secretary of the Communist party, Gomulka looked back on the events of the past and described his program for the future. He attacked Stalin's policies and denounced the terror in which so many "innocent people were sent to their death." He pledged to reform the Communist party (PZPR) so that members would have greater influence over decisions made by party leaders. Gomulka also reaffirmed his somewhat independent brand of Communism, the "Polish path to socialism":

> *Socialism is a social system eliminating man's exploitation and oppression by man . . . The roads to it . . . may differ . . . They are determined by various circumstances of time and place . . . Only through experience and through study of accomplishments of the various countries building socialism, can a model of socialism be created that best fits given conditions.*

The significance of the Polish October had been that Gomulka and the other Polish Communists would be allowed to exercise some independence. Khrushchev seemed content to let the PZPR run the country, and he did not intend to intervene in Polish affairs the way Stalin had done. But Gomulka and his associates had to tread carefully. If they became too independent of Moscow, they might suffer the fate of Hungary.

While being constantly concerned about Moscow, Gomulka also had to satisfy the demands of the Polish people. The Polish October had been the first time in a country controlled by the Communists that public opinion had forced a reform of the government. The Poles had supported Gomulka because they wanted him to end the nightmare of Stalinism, to improve the lagging economy, and to increase greatly the amount of freedom within Polish society. If Gomulka could not accomplish these things, he might be forced to resign, just as the man before him had been.

It was a dangerous tightrope Gomulka walked between the Soviet leaders and the Polish people. One false step and he could fall.

GOMULKA BEGINS

During the first years of his regime, Gomulka attempted to carry out a series of reforms. In the economic field, he put a halt to the policy of setting up agricultural collectives and allowed the workers to have a slightly greater role in running Polish industry. Censorship was reduced in the country. Certain books and magazines were permitted into Poland from the West, and some Polish writers were allowed to visit Western nations, including the United States.

Gomulka also changed the government's policy toward the Catholic church. He ordered Cardinal Wyszynski and other members of the clergy released from prison in 1956. In the future the church would be able to provide religious instruction in the schools and to publish its views more openly. This new policy did not mean that Gomulka agreed with the church's teachings. He was only practicing smart politics.

> . . . The idealist outlook [represented by the Catholic church] will persist alongside the materialist one [of the PZPR] for a long time. Thus there will be side by side the believers and nonbelievers, the church and socialism, people's government and the church hierarchy. From this fact we must draw the conclusions.

> In its policy [PZPR] cannot apply . . . pressure toward the believers, ignoring the fact that the old quarrel with the church had repelled millions of people from socialism.

During his return to power, Gomulka had criticized Stalin for not allowing the Polish parliament, Sejm, to have any power. In 1957 efforts were made to increase the role of Sejm in policy making. And the Polish legislature did achieve more influence than the legislatures of other Communist countries. However, the Sejm was controlled by a single party, the PZPR, so it could never be expected to act against the wishes of the Communist leaders.

So far Gomulka had permitted only a small increase in Poland's freedom. Yet his Soviet overlords were already criticizing him for going too far. They were also attacking his independent policy in foreign affairs. In 1956–1957 Gomulka established a firm relationship with Marshal Tito which continued despite sharp disagreements between Yugoslavia and the Soviet Union. At the same time Gomulka increased Poland's economic ties with the United States. In 1957 the Poles accepted a loan for $95 million and one for $97 million the following year. This brought a stinging attack from the Soviet newspaper *Pravda*. "The imperialists do not give anything away for nothing.

Everybody knows that American aid . . . leads . . . to economic and political dependence."

GOMULKA'S NEW DIRECTION

During the early part of his regime, Gomulka found himself becoming more and more isolated. He was losing the support of the Soviet Union for allowing too much freedom at home and showing too much independence abroad. In the meantime, he was also losing the support of the Polish people. Many Poles had expected Gomulka to carry out broad democratic reforms that would allow non-Communist groups to play a role in Poland's government. But so far he had done nothing.

Then in 1958 two events occurred that caused Gomulka to abruptly change direction. A fresh dispute broke out between the Soviet Union and Yugoslavia. All the other satellite countries backed the USSR. If Gomulka withheld his support, he would stand alone. At the same time Imre Nagy, leader of the Hungarian revolution, was executed by the Russians. Gomulka's position was clear: either he could back the Soviets, or face the same fate as Nagy.

A few months later Gomulka traveled to Russia for a visit with Khrushchev. Giving into Soviet pressure, he pledged his strong and continued support of the USSR. Thereafter Gomulka closely followed the Soviet line in foreign affairs as well as in domestic policies.

Gomulka's decision may seem like an abrupt turnaround in his political thinking, but in fact it fit nicely with his real political beliefs. Gomulka was a devoted Communist who never intended to bring broad democratic reforms to Poland or to do anything else that might undermine the position of the Communist party. The "Polish path to socialism" had been designed only to achieve some independence from Moscow. Once Gomulka realized his own position was in jeopardy, he bowed to the Soviets. He then took a series of steps designed to roll back many of the reforms of his early regime.

Gomulka put his own house in order by removing the more liberal members of the PZPR. They had advocated such measures as greater freedom for the press and less state control over the economy. At the same time Gomulka took back from the workers the power he had given them earlier to influence the running of local industry.

The Communist government also began an attack on the Catholic church. Catholic priests were prevented from ministering to church members in the hospitals, prisons, and armed forces. Catholic authorities were prevented from building new churches, their publications were censored, and religious gatherings of Catholic worshipers were disrupted. By 1960 the church had also been stopped from giving instruction in the schools.

Cardinal Wyszynski loudly denounced the policies of the Polish government. "People reach out for freedom," Wyszynski said, "and other people deprive them of it." Then he sent a warning to the government: "Woe to those who seek to deprive others of freedom."

The Communist attacks continued, and they were warmly supported by the Soviet leaders in Moscow; but Cardinal Wyszynski continued to speak out courageously in defense of freedom. In 1965 he said:

> Man is still regarded as the worst enemy of the state, as if the state were meant not for the people, but for itself . . . How long do we have to work until a citizen becomes a citizen in his own country, not a slave, not a prisoner all the time suspected, all the time shadowed, and somehow followed even in his innermost thoughts?

The Polish people supported their cardinal. Wyszynski was loudly hailed by an enormous crowd in the city of

Poznan when he came to celebrate an outdoor mass marking the one-thousandth anniversary of Catholicism in Poland. But at the same time only a short distance away, Gomulka spoke to a large gathering of Communists and accused Wyszynski of fighting "against People's Poland." He criticized the cardinal for not yielding "to the vital interests of the state."

Gomulka's policy of oppression spread to other areas of Polish society. Writers and intellectuals were censored, and their publications were seized by the government. In response, thirty-four of them signed a letter in 1964 stating that the Communists were "endangering the development of Polish national culture." They called on the Gomulka regime "to conform to the spirit of the rights guaranteed by the Polish Constitution and for the good of the nation." Gomulka cracked down on the writers even harder and arrested some of those who were behind the letter.

Even after the end of Stalin's terror, arrest and imprisonment remained powerful weapons which Gomulka did not hesitate to use against those who disagreed with him. The security police were everywhere—snooping, prying, ready to seize anyone who posed a threat, real or imagined, to the Communist regime.

The Gomulka era, which had begun amid such high hopes, had become a period of increasing repression. According to Adam Bromke, an expert on Polish affairs, many Poles dealt with this situation by turning away from politics and focusing on their own personal lives. Bromke points out that the Poles were especially concerned with their material welfare. The Polish people had always been drawn to Western culture, and into Poland came Western books, music, films, and fashions. Many Poles seemed to idolize the rich nations where people had automobiles and refrigerators. In Poland wages were low. Housing was scarce and there were far too few consumer items. As Bromke points out, the Poles "look [ed] for inspiration to the capitalist West. Communism still [had] little appeal in Poland."

This situation might well have given Gomulka reason to worry. For the West not only represented material wealth, it also championed the ideals of freedom and democracy. These ideals had threatened Gomulka before and he had suppressed them. But in 1968 they returned to threaten him once again.

REVOLUTION IN CZECHOSLOVAKIA

The situation in Czechoslovakia in 1967–1968 was similar to the one in Poland when Gomulka had come to power in 1956. The Czech government was controlled by autocratic Communist leaders who were under increasing fire from writers, students, and intellectuals who demanded more freedom. Finally the Communists selected a new, more liberal first-secretary named Alexander Dubcek. The Soviets hoped that Dubcek would be able to accomplish what Gomulka had done—satisfy the demands of the Czech people without going too far and letting things get out of control. That way, the position of the Communist party would remain secure, and Czechoslovakia wouldn't shake the Soviet empire.

But the Czechs were not going to be satisfied simply by a change in Communist leadership. Throughout the months that followed, they openly discussed the political future of their country, and Dubcek permitted these free and open discussions to proceed. Then in April the Central Committee of the Communist party adopted a new program in which they gave a share of their power to the Czech parliament, trade unions, and peasant groups. Press censorship was also eliminated. To the Soviet leaders, it looked like Poland all over again, and they warned Dubcek that he had gone too far.

Ironically, Gomulka was one of the loudest critics of

the Czech reforms. The man who had come to power promising the "Polish path to socialism" now attacked the Czech Communists when they asserted their independence. There were two reasons for Gomulka's position. First, he was carrying out his agreement of 1958 to follow the Soviet line. Since that time Gomulka had more than fulfilled his part of the bargain, and as a reward he had achieved a special place in the Soviet empire as a man who could always be trusted and relied on for support. Gomulka enjoyed this warm relationship with the Soviet leaders, and he wanted nothing to jeopardize it. Second, greater freedom in Czechoslovakia might undermine Gomulka's leadership at home. The Poles could easily decide to follow their Czech neighbors and unseat Gomulka because of his repressive policies.

Against all the opposition from the Soviets, the Poles, and the other Communist satellites, the Czechs continued with their revolution. In July they proclaimed their willingness to defend their newly-won freedoms, with force if necessary, against any foreign invasion. At this point the Soviets had heard enough. Although they had good reason to believe that the Czechs would not actually fight against a massive invasion, Soviet leaders could not take a chance that the Czech spirit of defiance might spread to other eastern bloc nations.

On August 21, 1968, the Russians invaded Czechoslovakia with an army of 400,000 including small units from the satellite countries. The Czechs put up almost no resistance. Their revolution was snuffed out almost before it began.

THE FALL OF GOMULKA

While Gomulka watched the situation in Czechoslovakia, a more serious crisis was brewing at home. In early 1968, the government censors banned a play because they said it was anti-Russian. The Polish writers protested, touching off a series of large student demonstrations at Warsaw University and at universities in other Polish cities. The students demanded a larger voice in running their institutions, they wanted greater democracy in Communist societies, and they expressed their solidarity with fellow students who were struggling for freedom in Czechoslovakia. The government security police put an end to the demonstrations, and the students went back to their classes. But for Gomulka the demonstrations of 1968 marked the beginning of the end.

Adam Bromke has compared Gomulka to Pilsudski who ruled Poland between the wars. Both were resistance fighters who had been in and out of prison. Both were Polish Nationalists, Bromke continues, and courageous men who were unafraid to defend their beliefs. But, Bromke concludes, as the years went on each man grew increasingly autocratic and far removed from his people.

Clearly, Gomulka had lost touch with writers, intellectuals, Catholics, and especially with the young. The younger generation strongly resented the restrictions which Gomulka had imposed on them. And, unlike some of their parents who had turned away from politics, many of the young were more prepared to express their beliefs and to challenge openly the regime, as the students had shown.

Gomulka also faced a challenge from inside the Communist party. One reason that some party members criticized Gomulka was due to his poor handling of the economy. There seemed to be too little emphasis placed on producing consumer items—cars and refrigerators—and too much emphasis on expanding heavy industry. The government had to import the machinery to power heavy industry, and it was forced to pay for these imports by exporting larger and larger amounts of food. As a result there were food shortages at home which bred anger and resentment among the Polish people.

Within the PZPR a group opposed to Gomulka had formed around Edward Gierek, a member of the Politburo, the party's governing body. Although born in Poland—the son of a coal miner—Gierek had been raised in France where he became a member of the French Communist party. Returning to Poland after World War II, he joined the PZPR, rising through the ranks to a position of leadership. Gierek was an efficient industrial manager and was seen by other party members as a man who could improve the Polish economy.

Gierek also presented a fresh alternative to Gomulka who, many party members believed, had clung to power far too long, and whose ideas seemed rooted in the past. Gomulka, like many of his cronies, was a hero of the war. But this period in Polish history was over. To a younger generation of Communists in their twenties and thirties, who hardly remembered the war, its heroes now seemed out of date. The younger Communists wanted an opportunity to run the party; and they felt themselves better qualified than the older generation, many of whom were not well educated. The younger Communists also believed they were more in touch with the needs of the Polish people. So they found themselves ready to support any change in the party that would give them greater control.

In December 1970 the government, bowing to severe economic pressures, raised food prices 30 percent. In Gdansk and other Baltic coast cities, the workers left their jobs in protest and began to demonstrate. Soon rioting broke out. To deal with these disturbances, Gomulka called out the army which brutally suppressed them. In the suppression of the workers, some were killed and many more were wounded.

Poles were stunned and seething with anger at Gomulka. The Communist leaders realized that this was the moment to act, and they removed Gomulka as first-secretary. Edward Gierek was selected to replace him.

THE AFTERMATH

The year 1970 looked like an instant replay of 1956. Once again the Polish people had taken to the streets. They had forced a change in the Communist government, and the Soviet Union had not intervened. The pendulum of Polish history had also swung once again. The years of calm and quiet, of turning away from politics had been replaced by a violent uprising.

In retrospect Gomulka had brought some progress to Poland. He had ended the Stalinist terror and freed the farmers from their collectives. Poland also maintained far greater contacts with the West than did the other satellite countries. But Gomulka seemed to promise far more than he ever delivered.

As first-secretary, Gomulka tried to balance the demands of his Soviet overlords, the Communist party, and the Polish people. He had satisfied the Soviets. He had failed to satisfy his own party and his people, who finally removed him. But the new Communist leaders had to be careful. They would also walk the same tightrope, and they could fall off just as Gomulka did.

CHAPTER IV
THE RISE AND FALL OF EDWARD GIEREK

When Gierek took over as first-secretary, Poland was reeling from the bloody riots in the cities along the Baltic coast. Gomulka's ruthless method of dealing with the demonstrators had given further proof to the Polish people of just how oppressive their government could be. This event brought renewed criticism from all the groups who were dissatisfied with the government: the church which had been demanding greater religious freedom; the intellectuals who wanted an end to censorship; the students and professors who wanted more influence in running their universities; the workers who were calling for higher wages; and every consumer throughout Poland who wanted to roll back price increases.

If Gierek ever hoped to govern effectively, he would immediately have to do some political "fence-mending" and regain the support of the Polish people. In a move designed to increase the government's popularity, the new first-secretary eliminated the price increases and announced a price freeze to last for two years. He went north to the Baltic seaports to meet with the Polish ship-yard workers. After hours of exhausting bargaining, the workers won an agreement from the government to raise wages.

Where Gomulka had remained aloof from the Polish people in recent years, Gierek now tried to establish closer contact with them. He traveled the country, meeting with factory workers, industrial managers, and local party officials. He had come, he said, to hear their complaints. Gierek also ordered members of his government to appear on television and answer questions from viewers about any of the issues that troubled them.

The new first-secretary made many promises calculated to appeal to the Polish people. He pledged to them a higher standard of living, saying that the government would place much greater emphasis on consumer items and less on heavy industry. He predicted that in a few years Poland would have plenty of cars and refrigerators and that there would be enough housing for everyone. Gierek also assured the Polish people that food shortages would end and that a long line at the market would eventually become a thing of the past.

In order to gain support from the Catholic church as well as from writers and intellectuals, Gierek readjusted the government's policy toward them. He gave Cardinal Wyszynski permission to build some new churches in Poland which the Gomulka regime had prevented. Censorship was reduced, allowing greater freedom not only to write, but also to read books which had previously been banned.

If all these proposals coming from the government sound familiar, they should. Gomulka had followed a similar program after assuming power in 1956. He too had attempted to assure the Polish people with promises and greater freedoms. Of course, the Poles were wary. They watched the Gierek government and waited to see how many of these promises the new first-secretary would actually carry out and how long it would be before he tightened the Communist grip once again.

OPENING TO THE WEST

To fulfill his promise to improve Poland's standard of living, Gierek turned to the West which had the technology necessary to modernize Polish industry and the consumer items which Poles desired. Gierek was permitted by his Soviet overlords to establish closer ties with western Europe, Canada, and the United States because a new atmosphere of détente now existed in East-West relations.

Détente, defined as a period of calm or relaxation, had resulted principally from circumstances affecting the United States and the USSR. Throughout the 1960s, the United States had been engaged in a terrible war in Vietnam. American presidents supported South Vietnam against attacks from the Communist government of North Vietnam, which had the backing of the Soviet Union. The war cost many American lives and many billions of American dollars, weakening the nation's economy. But the United States' efforts proved in vain. North Vietnam emerged victorious and united the country under Communist rule in 1973.

America entered the Vietnam War because of a commitment, first proclaimed in the Truman Doctrine, to defend free countries against the threat of Communism wherever it might appear in the world. But as the war intensified, many Americans came to question, and then oppose, this policy of being the world's policeman. As a result, U.S. leaders began to shape a new foreign policy which would be based on more peaceful relations with the Soviet Union and other Communist countries.

In the meantime, Soviet leaders had shown a greater interest in improving relations with the West. Within the Communist world a wide split had developed between the USSR and the Communist regime of China. Clashes between Russia and China had already occurred along their lengthy border. The Chinese were also trying to undermine the stability of the Russian empire. The necessity of dealing with the China situation made the Soviet leaders more anxious to reduce the risks of conflict with the West and promote the cause of peace. In addition Soviet leaders wanted to improve the Russian economy. Like Edward Gierek in Poland, they realized that to do this they needed Western technology and expertise.

The process of détente had already begun with agreements between the Soviet Union and the nations of France and West Germany. In 1970 West German Chancellor Willy Brandt formally reversed a long-standing policy of his country and accepted the division of Germany into east and west. In so doing, he recognized the existence of Communist East Germany, which the Soviets had established after World War II.

Over the next few years, a series of agreements worked out between President Richard Nixon and Soviet leader Leonid Brezhnev established détente between the two superpowers. In 1972 Nixon and Brezhnev met at a summit conference in Moscow where they agreed, among other things, to the principles of peaceful coexistence. Strategic Arms Limitation Talks (SALT) led to a treaty limiting nuclear weapons. The United States and the Soviet Union also agreed to expand trade and to share technology.

At the same time economic and political relations improved between the United States and Poland. In 1972 President Nixon visited Warsaw. The President and First-Secretary Gierek agreed to establish a joint commission which would expand trade between the two countries. In 1974 Gierek came to the United States where he signed declarations of "friendship" with American officials. Trade between the two countries continued to increase as Gierek sought to modernize the Polish economy.

ECONOMIC GAINS AND LOSSES

Gierek's economic policy called for the Polish government to import huge amounts of modern industrial machinery and consumer items from the West would be paid for by Polish exports, mainly food and coal. The Western nations were especially interested in Poland's coal because worldwide oil prices were rising due to the energy crisis.

Although the standard of living in Poland improved and industrial production, as well as wages, rose, severe problems quickly developed in Gierek's policy. The cost of Western imports greatly exceeded the revenues which the government received from its exports. Consequently, Poland began to pile up huge debts to its Western trading partners, which seriously undermined the strength of the Polish economy. The Polish government felt itself under increasing pressure to raise prices on goods within the country. But this kind of action was risky. In 1972 workers staged wildcat strikes protesting any increase in prices; the government, fearing a repeat of the events of 1970, rolled back the increases almost immediately.

In a different approach aimed at improving the economy, Gierek tried to increase food exports, but there too he encountered severe problems. Bad weather reduced the size of Poland's harvest in 1975. The country also lacked the mechanized equipment necessary to expand greatly its agricultural output. Efforts to produce more food for export and still feed Poland's large population led to food shortages.

In 1976 the government announced a large rise in food prices. The result was instantaneous. Polish workers went on strike throughout the country, and there was looting in Warsaw. Once again the government moved quickly to roll back the price increases. Gierek was also forced to send out a call for help to the Soviet Union, which shipped in food and consumer items to overcome the shortages inside Poland.

Throughout his attempts to change the Polish economy, Gierek constantly ran up against a spirit of independence among the Polish workers. They had not forgotten their role in bringing him to power, and their use of the strike was a constant reminder that they could remove him. This wasn't the only labor problem Gierek faced. Over and over again, Communist officials criticized the workers for absenteeism and the inferior quality of their production.

Following the strikes of 1976 the Gierek regime cracked down. Some strikers were arrested and later put on trial. Many others were fired from their jobs. But this just increased the Polish spirit of resistance. A group of intellectuals formed an organization called the Committee for Workers' Defense (KOR). They raised money to provide legal aid for the imprisoned strikers, as well as financial assistance for their families. Sometime later another organization began which called itself the Movement for Defense of Human and Civil Rights (ROPCIO). The members of this group exposed violations of human rights committed by the government against the strikers or anyone else in Poland.

Meanwhile a petition signed by 889 workers from a tractor factory near Warsaw had been sent to the government demanding that strikers fired from their jobs be rehired. The strikers' cause also received the support of Poland's powerful Catholic church. Catholic leaders criticized the government for its poor treatment of the workers, and protests against the Communist regime were held in various churches throughout the country. Bowing to intense pressure from so many groups, the government eventually released most of the imprisoned strikers in 1977.

OPPOSITION TO
THE GOVERNMENT

Efforts by intellectuals, workers, and church officials to gain the release of the strikers indicated the broad opposition to the government's policies. This opposition took many forms. There were demands by the workers for free trade unions. These unions had existed before the Soviet takeover; then the Communists seized control of them to stamp out opposition to their authoritarian regime. The Gierek government strongly opposed any new independent unions because "there are no and cannot be any antagonistic conflicts between the [present state-controlled] workers' organizations and the economic and state administration." Despite this opposition some free trade unions did spring into existence.

In the state-controlled universities students established independent unions, too. The unions continued to press long-standing student demands for greater influence over university policies. At the beginning of 1978 a group of professors formed an underground university to offer courses that were not permitted by the government. The university attracted a wide following among students until the Gierek regime sent the secret police to shut it down.

Gierek seemed to follow an inconsistent policy toward Polish desires for greater freedom. At times his regime acted ruthlessly, as in the case of the underground university. But in other cases the Communists seemed to retreat. In 1977, for example, government censors permitted the showing of a film called *Man of Marble* by the Polish director, Andrzej Wajda, which is highly critical of Communist society. Its hero is a Polish worker, exploited by the state, who supposedly dies in 1970 during the riots in Gdansk which were suppressed by Gomulka.

Throughout the 1970s, Poland's contacts with the

West continued. Each year the Polish government allowed far more students to study in Western countries than the Soviet Union did. In Warsaw and other Polish cities, young people could be seen wearing Western styles of dress. Western political ideas entered the country too, and the Gierek government found itself under increasing pressure to pursue more liberal policies.

In 1976 the government proposed a series of amendments to the Polish Constitution. One of the amendments would have recognized the Communist party as "the leading political force in the country." The second proclaimed Poland's "inseparable and unbreakable" alliance with the USSR. And the third stated that "citizens' rights are inseparably linked with honest fulfillment of their duties to the socialist motherland."

These amendments provoked strong opposition from broad segments of Polish society, including intellectuals and church leaders. They claimed that the government's action was in direct violation of a Helsinki agreement based on the Conference on European Security, signed by the United States and the USSR in 1975. The agreement called for both nations to respect "fundamental freedoms, including freedom of thought, conscience, religion or belief."

Critics of the proposed amendments pointed out that the Polish Constitution presently guaranteed a citizen's civil rights and these did not depend on fulfilling certain duties to the state. The critics also said that by emphasizing the country's permanent ties with the USSR, the government was violating Poland's sovereignty as a state.

Although Gierek could have tried to force the constitutional amendments on the Polish people, he chose instead to negotiate with the opposition groups. Such negotiations never would have occurred in a tightly controlled society like the Soviet Union. But the power of the opposition groups, especially the Catholic church, was so strong that Gierek could not ignore them.

Following a series of talks, a compromise was worked out and the government's amendments were changed. The Communist party became "a guiding political force in the construction of socialism." The amendment on civil rights said citizens must "honestly fulfill their duties toward the motherland." And the reference to Poland's "unbreakable" ties to the Soviet Union was eliminated.

STATE AND CHURCH

As the controversy over the Polish Constitution indicated, the Catholic church remained a potent institution. In a country of more than thirty million people, more than 90 percent are Catholic. Poles are fervent in their religious beliefs. Moreover, the Polish church is inseparably linked to the Poles' fierce spirit of nationalism. When Poland's Catholic primate, Stefan Cardinal Wyszynski, spoke it was not only as a religious leader, but as a national hero who commanded the loyalty of millions. Therefore, the Communists were forced to deal with the church very carefully.

In June 1977 Cardinal Wyszynski warned that a "Violation of human rights today . . . might give birth to new unrest tomorrow." Later that year Gierek held his first meeting with the Catholic leader since taking office in 1970. It was part of the government's effort to increase public goodwill after the constitutional crisis and the strikes of 1976. In line with this policy, Gierek also permitted construction of new Catholic churches, including the completion of one at Nowa Huta.

However, church officials continued to criticize the government and pressed for greater freedom. In 1978 they denounced government censorship, demanding "openness and free public opinion." They also called on the Communists to remove restrictions on Catholic publications.

In 1979, following his October 1978 election as Pope John Paul II, Karol Wojtyla returned to his native Poland. Before becoming Pope, Wojtyla had served as Archbishop of Krakow. Addressing vast multitudes of Catholics throughout the country, the Pope stated that "Christ cannot be kept out of the history of man in any part of the globe." He also called religious liberty a fundamental right. The Pope's remarks were strong indictment of Communist atheism and a direct challenge to the Gierek regime; while, at the same time, they stoked the fires of Polish nationalism.

GIEREK'S ECONOMIC
PROBLEMS CONTINUE

Among the Polish people, support for the government remained low. The Poles complained bitterly about increased shortages of everything from food and gasoline to clothes and other consumer items.

Following the 1976 riots, a government-backed report had predicted that the country was heading for economic catastrophe. The prediction seemed to be coming true. Poland's debts to the West continued to climb by billions of dollars. Just paying the interest on this debt cost the government so much that it could not afford the new machinery necessary to revitalize Polish industry or the consumer items demanded by the Polish people.

The Gierek regime took steps designed to deal with the worsening economy. It encouraged private enterprise in crafts and retail shops. The government also changed its agricultural policy. In the early seventies, Gierek had talked about increasing the number of collectives in Poland and began taking steps in that direction. This frightened Poland's independent farmers who withheld their produce from market, increasing the food shortages. Finally Gierek abandoned his plans for collectivization and reassured the farmers that their land was safe.

However, the food shortages did not disappear. The farmers could not produce enough to feed Poles at home and still provide the huge quantities necessary for export. The government faced another problem, too. It was caught between subsidizing the farmers, who charged market prices for their produce, and satisfying the Polish consumers, who demanded that food prices be kept artificially low. This cost the government billions in food subsidies at a time when it was already over-burdened with debts to the West.

Finally, in the summer of 1980 the Communist government found itself unable to afford the food subsidies any longer. On July 1, it announced a large increase in meat prices. The response of the Polish people was easily predictable. On July 2, workers in Warsaw protested the higher prices and called for pay raises.

Gierek held firm. He announced that the price increases would stay. And although promising some pay hikes, he told the workers that they would have to deal with the higher meat prices as best they could. The protests spread. Between July 15 and 17, 800,000 workers went on strike in Lublin. In Krasnik, workers at a ball-bearing plant staged a walkout. In a few days there were more than one hundred strikes throughout Poland, where strikes were prohibited by the Communist government.

Finally government officials gave in and announced higher pay rates. The strikers accepted the new wages and went back to work. Gierek had apparently weathered the crisis. But all the Poles were not satisfied. In early August, Warsaw municipal workers went on strike. Then, on August 14, shipyard workers in Gdansk took control of the Lenin shipyard. It was in this port city only ten years earlier that the workers had taken to the streets to protest higher food prices, only to be met by government troops who killed them. Would Gierek call out the army again?

At first, the Gierek regime only cut the communication lines to Gdansk. Meanwhile, the strikes had spread. In nearby Gdynia, workers walked off their jobs. By the middle of August strikes had broken out across the Baltic region. From their position inside the shipyard the workers presented the government with a list of demands, including

- the right to strike
- freedom of expression and abolition of censorship
- access by all religious groups to the mass media
- release of all political prisoners
- full supplies on the domestic market with only surpluses exported
- informing the public about the economic situation and permitting discussion of reforms
- reopening all communication links with Gdansk
- average salary increases of 2,000 zlotys ($65) for everyone
- publication on radio, television, and in the newspapers of information about the strikes
- the right to establish free trade unions

The Gierek regime refused to discuss these demands. Instead it took a hard line, rounding up seventeen members of the Committee for Workers' Defense (KOR), including one of its founders, Jacek Kuron. Almost a year earlier the KOR newspaper had issued a call to the workers to form independent trade unions. This, the paper said, will be "a power the authorities cannot ignore and will have to negotiate with on an equal footing." One of the people who signed this statement was Lech Walesa, who now led the strikers inside the shipyard.

On August 26, as the strikes in Poland showed no signs of ending, the government finally began to negotiate with Walesa and the other strike leaders at the Lenin shipyard. While the negotiations continued, Polish television—usually tightly controlled by the government—published progress reports and allowed the strikers to present their views. Debates over the future of Poland were also carried on in the media.

At last, on August 30, Walesa and his team reached an agreement with the government negotiators. The government agreed to allow independent trade unions, to pay strikers full salaries during the days they were on strike, to increase meat supplies and other commodities, to reduce censorship, and to increase wages. Under the terms of a similar pact signed in the city of Szczecin, the Communist regime also agreed to let the Catholic church broadcast in the media. In return the strikers pledged to recognize the leading role of the Communist party in Poland, not to form a political party of their own, and to honor all of Poland's alliances.

THE POLISH SUMMER
Walesa and the other strike leaders had scored a substantial victory, achieving what workers in no other satellite country had ever obtained—the right to form independent trade unions. In other eastern bloc countries all unions are controlled by the Communist Party. The agreements involving censorship and church access to the media, were also important because they promised to create an atmosphere of greater freedom.

For Gierek, the results of the August agreements were not so beneficial. Although he had succeeded in ending the strikes, he could not hold onto his job. In September the Communist party replaced him as first-secretary. Gierek shared the same fate as Gomulka for almost the same reasons. While satisfying his Soviet overlords, he failed to satisfy the Polish people. At the beginning of his regime, Gierek had promised the Poles that he would improve living standards. He expected his programs to revitalize the economy and bring prosperity. Then the Poles would not protest too loudly if he finally had to raise food prices. But there was no prosperity. And the Poles did protest— just as they had in 1970—sending Gierek the way of Gomulka.

Jozef Pilsudski, the leader of Poland during its brief period of independence between the two World Wars.

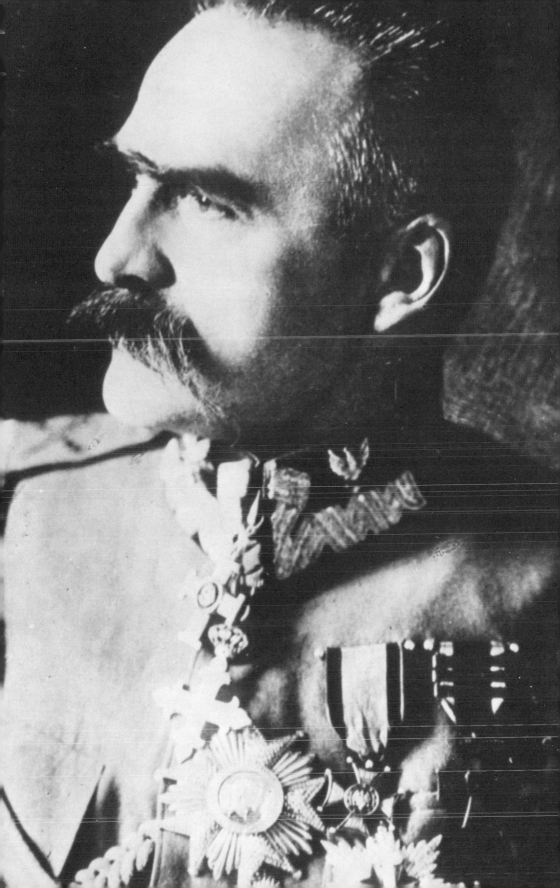

Above: relations between Wlaydslaw Gomulka (r.)
and Nikita Khrushchev (1.) improved significantly
after 1958 when the Polish leader abandoned
his attempt to achieve some independence
from Moscow. *Opposite:* following the uprising
by Polish resistance groups in Warsaw in 1944,
the Nazis declared that survivors, such as
these men, would be treated as prisoners
of war and sent to concentration camps.

Above: shortly after he became Pope John Paul II,
the former Polish Cardinal Karol Wojtyla (r.)
posed with his colleague, the greatly respected
Stefan Cardinal Wyszynski (l.). *Opposite:* striking
workers at the Lenin shipyard in Gdansk.

**Solidarity union leader Lech Walesa
talks with striking workers at
the Ursus tractor plant near Warsaw.**

The freer intellectual climate in Poland
made possible the return of the
exiled Nobel Prize-winning author
Czelaw Milosz (l.). Here he shares the
speakers' platform with Lech Walesa (r.) at
Lublin Catholic University in June 1981.

Above: long lines at supermarkets such as this large one in Gdansk have become a familiar sight in cities all over Poland as food shortages, high prices, and rationing continue to confront consumers. *Opposite:* delegates to the first National Congress of Solidarity met in Gdansk in September 1981 in the face of growing criticism from the Society Union and the Polish Communist party.

The day after martial law was imposed
in December 1981, armored cars such
as this one rolled through the streets
of Warsaw as soldiers stood guard.

CHAPTER V SOLIDARITY!

Stanislaw Kania was fifty-three when he became the new first-secretary in September, 1980. Kania had been a member of the Central Committee since the 1960s, and in 1970 he had been placed in charge of Poland's security affairs. Widely considered a conservative, he was known in party circles as an "apparatchik," a man who had made his career in the Communist bureaucracy.

In a speech before the Central Committee, Kania announced that he intended to maintain a low profile as the new leader. "I am not sure that our party needs what is usually termed a leader," he said. "I am deeply convinced that my obligation should above all consist in insuring that the collective wisdom of people should govern."

Kania was critical of the party's past policies, admitting that the recent crisis had resulted from "serious economic mistakes." This was the type of statement that Communists did not often make. In an effort to reassure the Soviet leaders who were watching the crisis, Kania said: "Our alliance with the Soviet Union has paramount importance for the security and economic wealth of the country." Finally, Kania pledged to carry out the agreements made at Gdansk with the Polish workers. He promised to improve the housing situation in Poland, where severe shortages still existed, to reduce censorship, and to increase democracy. "We shall take care that all . . . agreements be implemented. Democracy is not a gesture of the ruling power towards society, but it is a great need of society."

Polish leaders took a number of steps designed to restore calm and stability inside the country. One high government official flew to Moscow, reportedly to tell President Brezhnev that Poland's Communists were firmly in control of the situation. This was not a repetition of events in Hungary or Czechoslovakia. Brezhnev gave his support to the new Communist leadership and offered food and consumer items to help the Polish government deal with worsening economic conditions.

Meanwhile, Kania went on a tour of the country, stopping at factories and coal mines where he spoke to thousands of Polish workers. He repeated his promises that the August agreements would be kept and the party would recognize the workers' right to form independent trade unions. Admittedly, this was a difficult pill for the Communists to swallow. As Adam Bromke points out, "It undermines the legitimacy on which Communist power rests, by refuting the claim of the Communist Party to be the sole, authentic representative of the working class."

Poland's workers were understandably skeptical. They had listened to promises in the past from Gierek and Gomulka—promises that had been broken. But this time they intended to force the government to carry out its agreements.

SOLIDARITY FORMS
In September 1980 Poland's independent trade unions came together and registered with the government as a single organization calling itself Solidarity. In a speech before union members in Warsaw, Lech Walesa pointed

out the power possessed by a single union. "If there are difficult problems we can all strike together," he said. "If things get bad we stand together as a united Poland."

Masses of workers had already begun defecting from the Communist-controlled trade unions to join Solidarity. There seemed little the government was able to do to stop them, although Walesa complained that the Communists used every opportunity to harass Solidarity's recruitment efforts. Nevertheless, Solidarity prevailed, and, by the end of the year, had grown to over ten million—the vast majority of Poland's workers.

Solidarity's most potent weapon was the strike. The workers had used it over and over in the past to force the government to roll back food prices and grant wage increases. And Solidarity's leaders were prepared to use the strike again when they believed the Communists might not carry out their agreements.

In October, Walesa announced a one-hour "warning strike," and millions of workers throughout Poland walked off their jobs. The strike had been called, Walesa said, because of government delays in granting promised wage increases and freedom of the press, and in allowing Solidarity access to the media. The Communists claimed that they were carrying out all the agreements that had been signed in August. However, the warning strike served notice on the government: if it did not move according to Solidarity's timetable, the union could easily call a much longer strike that would cripple the economy and seriously undermine the Communist party's ability to rule.

Meanwhile a dispute broke out over Solidarity's charter. A Polish judge had ruled that the charter must include a statement recognizing the "leading role" of the Communist party. Although union leaders had seemingly agreed in August to accept the party's position in Poland, they had not written it into their charter. In response to the judge's decision, Solidarity leaders threatened a nation-wide strike for early November. Eventually the government backed down and the Polish Supreme Court ruled that the main body of Solidarity's charter would not have to mention the supremacy of the party. But the party's "leading role" would have to be included in the charter's annex, tacked on the end.

Walesa claimed a major victory against the government in the union's struggle for independence. "We have achieved what we wanted," he said. "We have won what we set out for on August 31." Ironically, the Communist government also claimed victory for getting the statement into the charter annex.

FREEDOM IN THE AIR

The spirit of freedom being demonstrated by Poland's workers was affecting other areas of Polish life, too. Under the terms of the agreements reached in August, the Catholic church began broadcasting religious services over the state-controlled radio. On the occasion of the first broadcast, Bishop Jerzy Modzelewski called it a "memorable hour" which "enriches our enormous religious and national feelings." The bishop went on to say that "the Polish Church rejoices and expresses its joy." Then, in the words of Christ, he proclaimed: "You shall know the truth and the truth shall make you free."

Greater freedom was gradually coming to the cultural and intellectual life of Poland. The country began to experience a period of *odnowa*, or renewal. The underground universities, which had been suppressed in the past, began to grow stronger. Government censorship of films was slowly relaxed. For the first time a newsreel appeared which showed the army's brutal attack on the strikers during the riots of 1970. Literature, which had been banned for being critical of Communism, could now be read. Even the Sejm, Poland's parliament, began to assert its independence from Communist domination. Some parliament members called on the government to defend its economic policy which had proven so disastrous for the country.

While the freedom movement in Poland had been started by the workers and owed its continued existence largely to the threat of the strike, it was spreading to embrace other segments of society. Strong links had been formed among Solidarity, the intellectuals, and the Catholic church. As the movement grew it became more powerful, but it also encountered growing pains.

SOLIDARITY'S LEADER

Following the victory at Gdansk, Lech Walesa became a national hero. In his trips throughout Poland, the workers hailed their new leader, chanting his nickname: "Leszek! Leszek!" His picture appeared in the press not only inside the country, but in many parts of the world. Walesa had become an international celebrity.

Yet, very little was known of this man who had risen from relative obscurity. Walesa had participated in the workers' movement during the riots of 1970 and the strikes of 1976. He had also served in the labor underground organizing workers against the government. And clearly he possessed the charisma and abilities of a natural leader. Like other popular leaders, Walesa seemed to thrive in his new position. According to one source, he considered himself a "man of destiny" whom God had selected to lead his people.

However, it remained unclear to many observers where Walesa had chosen to lead the millions who now followed him. In August at Gdansk he had been prepared to compromise with the government and settle for less than the workers were demanding. But when they accused him of "selling out," he immediately changed his position.

On one occasion in October Walesa cautioned the workers against calling strikes and pushing the government too hard for too many concessions. Then, a few weeks later, he threatened a nationwide strike over the wording of Solidarity's charter. This reportedly displeased some workers who were reluctant to walk off their jobs over such an issue.

As Solidarity's leader, Walesa walked a thin line, and there were signs that his initial popularity might be declining as he tried to satisfy the demands of a large union whose members often disagreed. On one side were the more radical members, led by men such as KOR founder Jacek Kuron, who wanted to press the government harder. Some of the radicals were reportedly unhappy over the charter issue when Solidarity had to include the statement, even in the annex, recognizing the "leading role" of the Communist party. On the other side was a group of moderate leaders, including Catholic intellectuals, writers, and church leader Cardinal Wyszynski. Walesa may have sought the cardinal's advice before his negotiations with the government over the charter.

Observers reported that Walesa often vacillated between the moderates and the radicals—between the willingness to compromise and the inclination to call a nationwide strike. However, no one seemed to know much more about him. What were Walesa's political ideas? What future did he have in mind for Solidarity and Poland?

In one interview Walesa said he believed in democracy, which would mean enormous changes in Poland's political system. Yet Walesa also claimed that he did not want to change the government. Did this mean that Walesa saw Solidarity playing the role of a powerful pressure group which would make the government more responsive to the needs of the people? Or did he envision Solidarity becoming a political party, as some of the radicals had urged, and sharing power with the Communists? Such a move, however, would undermine Communist control and might eventually lead to Soviet intervention.

THE PROBLEMS OF
KANIA AND WALESA

While Walesa was guiding Solidarity, his chief political adversary, First-Secretary Stanislaw Kania, was trying to lead the Polish Communist party through possibly the worst crisis in its history. Both men faced remarkably similar problems.

Upon becoming first-secretary, Kania had to deal with a Communist party sharply divided. Kania moved quickly to consolidate his power by removing members of the Central Committee who were supporters of Edward Gierek. But he still faced strong opposition among hard-liners who wanted him to take a tougher stand against Walesa. At the local level, party members also disagreed over how far the government should go in granting reforms.

An even more serious problem shared by Kania and Walesa was the declining Polish economy. The wage increases negotiated at Gdansk were a tremendous burden for the government which already found itself in dire financial straits. Debts to the West continued to mount. The government lacked the funds to pay its Western creditors or even to keep Poland's industries in full operation. A Communist regime was supposed to guarantee its people full employment, yet ten thousand workers had to be laid off at an automobile plant because auto parts were not available.

Meanwhile, farmers suffered another bad harvest. Food exports to the West had to be reduced and eventually eliminated. At home shortages grew worse as long lines formed at the markets. Finally the government was forced to introduce meat rationing. The production of coal—Poland's other big export—was also down as a result of shorter work hours.

A third problem faced by Walesa and Kania was the Soviet Union. In September 1980 Brezhnev had congratulated Kania on his appointment as party leader. But as the crisis continued, Moscow's concern grew. During the conflict over Solidarity's charter, Kania and Polish Prime Minister Jozef Pinkowski flew to Moscow for a meeting with Brezhnev. Afterward the Soviets issued a statement expressing their belief that the "working people of fraternal Poland" would work out the "acute problem of political and economic development facing them." According to reliable diplomatic sources, these words really meant that Moscow was watching the situation in Poland very carefully and might take action if the crisis grew worse.

Following this conference Kania returned to Warsaw where he and Walesa met for the first time. After their meeting Walesa asked the Polish workers to show moderation and called for an end to the wildcat strikes which had been occurring without his approval.

Then another crisis erupted. Police entered Solidarity's Warsaw headquarters and arrested two men who were charged with stealing a secret document which described how the Communist government dealt with dissenters. When word of the arrests got out, sixteen thousand workers at the Ursus tractor plant near Warsaw went on strike and refused to return to their jobs until the two men were released. Strikes spread to other parts of Poland. Some members of Solidarity demanded a complete investigation of police methods and stricter control of their activities.

Walesa met with government officials, and eventually they negotiated a compromise. The two men were immediately released, and the government agreed to hold future discussions on police tactics. Walesa also promised no more strikes for six weeks.

The compromise did not please many union members who wanted much more. But after hours of talking, Walesa finally convinced them that if they pressed the government too hard this time, they might bring down Soviet "tanks and rockets."

THE SOVIETS TAKE ACTION

The Soviet Union had already decided that the crisis in Poland had gone far enough. Soviet leaders had lost patience with the continuing demands made by Solidarity and believed that the Polish Communists had failed to deal with the union effectively. In November the Soviets began to mass troops along Poland's borders. They seemed ready to launch an invasion.

The Central Committee of the Polish Communist party reacted immediately. In a statement addressed to the Polish people, the committee said: "Countrymen, the fate of the nation and the country hangs in the balance." The Soviets hurriedly called a meeting of the Warsaw Pact nations in the Polish capital. At the conference, First-Secretary Kania reaffirmed the loyalty of Poland to the Soviet alliance. In return the Pact members pledged "fraternal solidarity and support." They agreed to insure the security of Poland while allowing the Polish Communists to safeguard Communism within the country.

Did this mean that the Soviets had decided to call off the invasion? Soviet troops still remained poised on Polish borders. The United States and other Western countries warned the Soviets about the consequences of invasion. The foreign ministers of NATO said that military intervention would jeopardize relations with Russia. The Western allies also agreed to impose economic sanctions on the USSR.

Inside Poland there were calls for national unity and an end to political conflict. Although Solidarity continued pressing the government to expand civil liberties, the union adopted a more moderate approach. In urging the release of four dissidents, Solidarity leaders did not threaten a strike, but decided instead to form a committee to study the matter. The Catholic church condemned those extremists whose acts "could raise the danger of a threat to the freedom and statehood of the fatherland." In a stern warning to the Soviets, the speaker of the Sejm said Poland would not allow "any intervention from the outside." But the Soviet armies did not intervene. And the crisis passed.

Many foreign affairs analysts speculated as to why the Soviets had decided against invasion. Some compared the Polish situation to the Hungarian crisis of 1956. The Soviets had attacked Hungary only after the Hungarian Communist party had withdrawn from the Warsaw Pact. That had not occurred in Poland.

Yet other analysts pointed out that when the Soviets invaded Czechoslovakia in 1968, it was still a member of the Warsaw Pact. In this case, the Soviets believed the Czech Communist party had lost control of the country. They also feared that the Czech revolution might spread to other satellites. Some observers believed that the Soviets might have been reluctant to invade because they were already involved in a war in Afghanistan. Soviet armies had invaded that country in 1979 to protect Russia's southern border and prop up a shaky Communist regime.

However, Poland occupies an even more strategic position in central Europe astride communications between the USSR and East Germany. The Soviets could never permit Poland to slip from their grasp—no matter what the cost. The Soviets fully realize that the cost of invasion would be extremely high. Unlike the Czechs, the

Poles are prepared to fight. A conflict in Poland would involve a major Soviet commitment of men and money. And, after the conflict had ended, the Soviets would be faced with ruling a rebellious people, seething with anger and hatred.

If the Soviets invade, they also would be forced to deal directly with the Polish economy. Coal production is down, food remains in short supply, and Poland's debts to the West total about $20 billion. A war in Poland would further weaken the economy and make the job of rebuilding it even harder. The Soviet Union already has enough economic problems at home without taking on Poland's.

The Soviets may conclude that the political situation in Poland has not yet become grave enough to undertake a bloody invasion and assume the burden of dealing with Poland's unruly people and shaky economy. Soviet leaders also may be unwilling to do further damage to East-West relations which would certainly worsen following an invasion. Détente had already been seriously undermined by Soviet actions in Afghanistan and elsewhere. U.S. officials have made it clear that an attack on Poland would result in serious economic and political countermeasures. The Soviets continue to rely heavily on Western technology for their industries and grain to feed their people. If these supplies are cut off, it would jeopardize the Soviet economy.

Although the Soviet invasion did not occur, the threat remained. The Soviets had clearly indicated to Walesa what could happen if Solidarity pushed too far. And they had shown Kania what could result if the Polish Communists let the country slip from their control.

CHAPTER VI FROM RENEWAL TO REPRESSION

Despite the ever-present threat of Russian military intervention, the Poles continued to assert their independence through 1981. A major source of contention between the government and Solidarity was the length of the workweek. Poles had been used to working a six-day, forty-six-hour week. Solidarity wanted this changed to five days and forty hours. The government refused; but Solidarity declared Saturdays work-free anyway in January 1981. Workers took Saturdays off despite government fears that it would reduce productivity. Finally, in January, Walesa called a series of brief warning strikes in various cities in an attempt to force the government to permit shorter hours of employment. At this point the Communists capitulated and agreed "in principle" to a forty-two-hour workweek including one Saturday per month.

Solidarity had won a major victory. But its effect on the Polish economy would be severely damaging. In the Polish area of Silesia lie some of the largest coal deposits in Europe—an estimated 120 billion tons. In 1979 Poland exported forty million tons of this coal which helped substantially in paying off the country's debt to the West. But the reduced workweek meant that Polish coal miners produced about 20 percent less coal for export.

Eventually, Solidarity agreed to allow the miners to work voluntarily on Saturdays. Yet it was unclear just how many did, even though the government offered them extra pay. Miners had very little incentive to earn more money because severe shortages of food and consumer items meant that there was nothing to buy.

The problem in the coal mines was a sad illustration of the terrible state of Poland's entire economy. While wages increased in 1981 as a result of the agreements of Gdansk, the production of food and industrial goods declined. At Solidarity's insistence meat and other foods were rationed so everyone could get a fair share of the short supplies.

Meanwhile, Poland's debts to the West continued to rise. As one government official said: "It's sad we have to spend so much repaying debts when we need raw materials and semifinished products for our industry." An example of industry's plight was a state-owned Polish television factory which had agreed to produce TV sets for the American market. The factory was unable to fulfill its agreement because it lacked parts—the government couldn't afford to buy them.

Poland's Western creditors took a variety of measures designed to improve the country's economic situation. They agreed to delay the repayment of Poland's debts, to guarantee new loans to the Polish government, and to provide food supplies at low prices. They also pressed the Communist government to accept a new economic program. This included a heavier investment in agriculture, while abandoning certain industrial enterprises which had not been productive. In addition the program called for less direction of the economy by the central government and more autonomy for local factory managers. Too much central control had led to economic mistakes. Finally, the program included an increase in prices.

Of course, no economic plan could go into effect without Solidarity's approval. Not surprisingly, the rank-and-file continued to oppose price increases. However, an agreement was finally reached under which workers' councils and the government would jointly name factory managers in certain industries. This type of system already existed in Yugoslavia and Hungary. But it was new in Poland and gave the workers a far greater degree of "self-management" than they had been permitted in the past.

Incidentally, many Communists felt the government had gone too far and allowed the workers too much self-management. On the other hand, many of Solidarity's members felt Walesa should have pushed the government harder and forced it to give the workers greater control in the factories.

THE RISE OF
RURAL SOLIDARITY

As the workers' movement grew more powerful, Poland's independent farmers began to organize, too. In the southeastern region of the country, farmers staged a warning strike in protest against government attempts to prevent them from forming their own union, which they called Rural Solidarity. The farmers' cause received strong support from Walesa and church leaders, including Cardinal Wyszynski. The Catholic primate said: " . . . farmers must be guaranteed security and stability, and their right to free assembly as unions must be recognized."

Under increasing pressure, the Communist government retreated and allowed the farmers to form an "association" but not a union. The farmers were extremely angry. But Walesa and Cardinal Wyszynski persuaded them to accept the compromise, at least temporarily. At this time Pinkowski was replaced as prime minister by Defense Minister General Wojciech Jaruzelski. A short time later the farmers began demonstrating again, demanding that the government grant recognition to their union. One of these demonstrations was forcibly broken up by the authorities, who injured some of the farmers.

This incident, together with other issues, created a major crisis. In March 1981 Walesa demanded that the government conduct an investigation to find out who was responsible for injuring the farmers. He also called on the government to recognize Rural Solidarity, to give the unions greater access to the media, and to free political prisoners who had supported the union movement. When the government did not grant these demands, Walesa called a four-hour warning strike, and throughout Poland millions of people walked off their jobs.

There were fears that Walesa might have gone too far this time. Some Western experts believed that Kania would impose martial law on the country, or the Soviets would intervene. But in the end a compromise was worked out. The government agreed to punish those responsible for injuring the farmers and to establish a commission to examine the question of recognition for Rural Solidarity.

In only a few weeks the Communists had given in completely and announced that the farmers could form their own union. Rural Solidarity leader Jan Kulaj called this decision a "great victory." The government realized that only by granting the farmers' demands could it hope to increase agricultural production and overcome food shortages.

SOME BARRIERS FALL

Demands for greater freedom were not limited to workers and farmers. At the university in Lodz, four thousand students staged a sit-in, demanding that the government allow them to draw up a new curriculum and establish their own union free of Communist control. Similar demonstrations occurred in the universities at Warsaw and Poznan. Since the Kania government already had enough problems with the declining economy and the labor strikes, it granted the students the right to set up an independent organization. Students at Warsaw University were permitted to publish a newspaper free of government censorship.

In 1981 censorship slowly continued to decline. Solidarity had already achieved the right to publish its own newspaper. Archbishop Jozef Glemp, the new Polish Primate,[1] said that it was "inadmissible to limit freedom of speech only because the proclaimed views may contain a truth which is uncomfortable for somebody." He called for greater access to the media, saying that all "social groups should make use of the mass media which is social property and should serve the whole society."

After thirty years in exile, Nobel Prize–winning author Czelaw Milosz returned to Poland and received a hero's welcome. The return of Milosz, like the visit of Pope John Paul II in 1979, increased the spirit of Polish pride and nationalism, encouraging the Poles to continue their struggle. Nevertheless, observers noted that Poles did not seem agreed on where they wanted that struggle to take them and who they wanted to lead them there.

WALESA AND SOLIDARITY

Lech Walesa still symbolized for millions the rebirth of Poland. But he could never satisfy all the hopes which the Poles had placed in him. Farmers, students, clergy, workers—everyone expected his support. There was bound to be disappointment and disillusionment.

[1] Glemp replaced Wyszynski as Primate of Poland after the latter's death on May 28, 1981.

Within Solidarity some members had already grown tired of his leadership. Many others simply resented authority, whether it was exercised by Walesa or some other leader. They had taken a measure of power from the Communists, and they were not about to hand it over to someone else. Solidarity was never a single, unified union tightly controlled from the top, but a collection of local unions that often acted on their own. And the locals wanted to keep it that way.

This explains the wildcat strikes that occurred so frequently in Poland. At Lodz, for example, 300,000 workers called a one-hour warning strike because five union activists had been fired from their jobs. After the workers threatened a much longer walk-out, Walesa and Poland's new prime minister, General Wojciech Jaruzelski, held a negotiating session to deal with the situation. Eventually, the two men worked out an agreement allowing the activists to return to work.

One crisis had ended. But another strike broke out in Radom where workers were demanding that several local Communist officials be removed from their positions. In August workers walked off their jobs in Warsaw over food shortages. Once again Walesa met with government officials, but they failed to find any way of solving the problem. Although the workers returned to their jobs, they were clearly disappointed. Wildcat strikes protesting food shortages continued throughout the year.

In his dealings with the Communist government, Walesa continued to follow the same policy—alternating between brinksmanship and conciliation. He would push the Communists hard for concessions as he had in March, taking Poland to the brink of war with the Soviet Union. Then, at other times, he demonstrated a desire to get along with the Communists.

In a speech to automobile workers in Warsaw, Walesa said that the government had been forced to deal with many difficult problems in Poland and should be given a chance to solve them. When Russian war memorials were defaced, Walesa condemned the action and offered to clean them. He also called on union members to stop striking over food shortages and the imprisonment of political dissidents.

Walesa realized how important it was to establish a working relationship with Kania and Jaruzelski, both of whom were considered moderates. If he pressed these men too far and forced them to grant too many concessions, they might be replaced by Communist hard-liners.

In September, however, the spirit of compromise seemed to disappear when Solidarity opened the first part of its National Congress in Gdansk. The congress passed a series of resolutions calling for free and democratic elections to parliament, freer access to the mass media, reforms in schools and revisions of Communist-inspired history textbooks, and freedom for political prisoners. Finally the congress sent a message to workers in other Communist bloc countries urging them to form independent trade unions.

This message enraged the Soviet Union which labeled the National Congress an "anti-Soviet orgy." Kremlin leaders believed that Solidarity was trying to encourage rebellion in the other bloc countries and to undermine the Soviet empire. It was this same belief that prompted the Russian invasion of Hungary and Czechoslovakia.

In a continuing attack on Solidarity, Soviet television showed Russian workers condemning the union. Steelworkers stood with banners saying "We will defend socialism in Poland." In a letter to the Poles, Soviet workers called Solidarity "counterrevolutionary and anti-socialist," and accused it of planning to seize power in Poland. Other Communist countries joined in the attack, harshly criticizing events in Poland and calling on the country to set its house in order.

The Polish Communists declared that Solidarity was trying to become a political party. This, the Communists said, would result in a "new national tragedy" creating a "confrontation threatening bloodshed."

Despite continuous verbal attacks from the Communists inside and outside the country, Solidarity reconvened later in the fall for the second part of its National Congress. At this session KOR, the radical group, formally disbanded. Since KOR had not been active in recent months, the move was really a symbolic gesture designed to show that radical elements did not control the union.

Solidarity made proposals on a broad range of issues that were supposedly the sole responsibility of the Communist government. These included foreign affairs, military spending, health, environmental protection, and inflation. Finally, the union elected Lech Walesa as its leader.

THE FORTUNES OF
STANISLAW KANIA

While Walesa remained the leader of Solidarity, Stanislaw Kania's position as head of the Communist party seemed to grow more unstable. Like his predecessors, Gierek and Gomulka, Kania had to juggle the expectations of the Polish people, the Communists in his own party, and the Soviets. It was extremely difficult for any politician to succeed. The Soviets had directed Kania repeatedly to take a stronger stand against Solidarity. On more than one occasion Russian armies seemed ready to invade Poland because Kania had been unable to control the situation there.

In June, at a meeting of the Polish Communist Central Committee, Kania faced a tremendous challenge from the hard-liners. The Soviets had recently sent Kania a harsh letter condemning him for letting Polish radicals destroy the country. The letter also stated: "There has been a serious change in the relationship [between Soviet and Polish leaders]. Now there has been an open split." The message seemed clear: the Soviets wanted Kania replaced; and the hard-liners tried to oust him. At the Central Committee meeting, they attacked Kania for constantly yielding to Solidarity's demands and failing to solve the country's problems. According to political writer Tad Szulc, the hard-liners called for a vote to remove Kania. Although they may have possessed a majority, the vote was temporarily postponed.

Then, Szulc reports, Kania and his associates went to work gathering support to keep him in power. They talked to Poland's top military leaders, who were also members of the Central Committee. They reminded the generals that, with Kania gone, the hard-liners might resort to repression to deal with the present crisis. This would only provoke Solidarity and eventually would lead to civil war between the army and the Polish people. The generals were extremely reluctant to risk bloodshed. When the Central Committee finally voted on Kania, they backed him and he retained his position.

In July Kania presided over the Communist party congress in Warsaw. The Communists had caught the same spirit of democracy as the rest of Poland's citizens. According to new rules, which Kania had been forced to approve, delegates to the congress were selected by secret ballot following election contests involving several candidates. Nothing like this had ever happened before in the Communist party.

At the congress delegates also cast secret ballots for members of the Central Committee. And, instead of following the traditional practice of letting the committee select the first-secretary, the delegates insisted on selecting him. They wanted to exert greater control over the Communist leadership. When the balloting for first-secretary finally occurred, Kania was reelected by a huge margin.

Once again Kania had succeeded in holding onto his leadership. But then came Solidarity's congress in September and the demand for more reforms. This was quickly followed by new directives from the Soviet Union telling Kania to crack down on Solidarity. In late September the Politburo in Warsaw considered a series of measures that would have imposed martial law on the country and could have resulted in fighting. Hard-liners reportedly favored the measures. But Kania and other moderates were opposed and prevented them from ever going into effect.

One reason for Kania's position may have been the knowledge that harsh action would not be supported by rank-and-file Communists. Many party members belonged to Solidarity. If a conflict broke out, Kania feared their first loyalty would be to the union.

Nevertheless, the first-secretary did not hesitate to mount a verbal assault against Solidarity. At a meeting of the Central Committee in October 1981, Kania said that all strikes should be suspended "for the common good." He accused radicals in Solidarity of trying to disrupt Poland's economy "in order to create conditions for taking over political power."

Yet Kania still offered a small concession. He and other Communist leaders spoke of expanding the National Unity Front to include members of Solidarity and the church. The front is a political group, dominated by the Communists, which selects members to serve in parliament.

This proved to be Kania's last proposal as first-secretary. Party leaders believed he had yielded too often to the demands of Solidarity and, in the process, had lost too much respect for the Communist party. Moreover, none of his proposals had been able to solve Poland's worsening economic crisis. Kania had also succeeded in antagonizing Moscow. As new first-secretary, the Central Committee chose General Wojciech Jaruzelski, who continued to hold the position of prime minister, as well as minister of defense. Jaruzelski became the first general to govern Poland since Pilsudski.

At fifty-eight, General Jaruzelski was a career military man who had been trained in Moscow and had fought with the Soviets during World War II. Although he had the support of the Kremlin, Jaruzelski was considered a moderate. In 1970 he had refused to support Gomulka's use of force to suppress the demonstrations. Appointed prime minister by Kania in February 1981, Jaruzelski seemed to hold many of the same political beliefs. Yet the General combined a willingness to compromise with a reputation for firmness, which Communists hoped would be the right combination for dealing with Poland's problems.

THE GENERAL CRACKS DOWN

Shortly after becoming first secretary in the autumn of 1981, Jaruzelski sent army units to towns and villages throughout the country. The government announced that this action had been taken to assure a smooth flow of food and other consumer goods to the Polish people. But it was also seen as a show of strength by the Communist authorities. At the same time General Jaruzelski seemed ready to embrace a policy of reconciliation. In November he sat down with Lech Walesa and Archbishop Glemp to discuss methods of improving Poland's economic problems. It was the first time the three leaders had officially met.

Then, on Saturday December 12, a new crisis arose. At a meeting in Gdansk, the Solidarity leaders took a radical step. They called for a national referendum on establishing a non-Communist government in Poland and changing the country's military relationship with the Soviet Union under the terms of the Warsaw Pact. This action did not have the support of Lech Walesa.

General Jaruzelski struck without warning. On December 13, 1981, he declared martial law, suspended Polish civil liberties and announced that the military had taken over the government. Solidarity was no longer permitted to operate. In a series of lightning police raids, the union's leaders were rounded up throughout Poland and thrust into prison. Lech Walesa was reportedly placed under house arrest. Jaruzelski also ordered the arrest of former Communist leaders, including former First Secretary Edward Gierek. In addition Catholic priests were reportedly jailed and beaten. All strikes and demonstrations were banned, and anyone who the government believed to be suspicious could be arrested immediately.

The government's crackdown was so swift and so well coordinated that it had obviously been planned far in advance. The Communists had only been waiting for the right moment. Jaruzelski's actions had apparently come only after consultation with the Soviet Union, and they had the full support of Moscow.

Solidarity called on the Polish people to oppose the government with a general strike. But it never materialized. Scattered strikes that did break out at some plants were broken up by Polish armed forces. In Warsaw, riot police stormed the Huta Warsjawa steel mill and took control of it from striking workers. Clashes between troops and coal miners in Silesia led to the deaths of some miners and injuries to many others. Shipyard workers in Gdansk were also injured when troops broke up their demonstrations.

The situation inside Poland was watched carefully by the United States and its Western allies. The Reagan Administration cut off economic aid to Poland. In a strongly worded statement the U.S. vowed that "the use of violence against the Polish people by the government would have extremely grave consequences."

TOWARD THE FUTURE

The events of December 1981 seemed to mark an abrupt end to the Polish renewal that had begun in Gdansk sixteen months earlier. Solidarity had always faced the threat of possible government repression or Soviet intervention. Yet, for a time, the union seemed to lead a charmed existence. It pushed continually for greater freedom for all segments of Polish society, and each time the Communist government seemed to yield. Finally the end came. Surprisingly, the leaders of Solidarity were caught completely off guard.

What the future holds for Solidarity—and the rest of Poland—is difficult to determine. This much is certain: the country still faces a grave economic crisis. Unless food shortages can be eliminated, industrial production increased, and the crushing debts to the West reduced, life for the Poles will remain very bleak.

Other questions concerning Poland are much harder to answer. Can we expect a mass movement like Solidarity to simply disappear, or will some form of it remain? Have all the freedoms won during the Polish renewal been lost indefinitely, or will some of them eventually be reinstated? Will there be more bloody clashes between the government and the Polish people, or will Poles accept the repressive measures imposed on them?

During the many years of foreign occupation, Poles have staged repeated revolts that have been snuffed out by the authorities. For a time Poles have submitted and become politically inactive only to revolt and begin the process of national renewal all over again. Perhaps this historical pattern will provide some answers to the future of Poland.

BIBLIOGRAPHY

Bromke, Adam. *Poland's Politics: Idealism vs. Realism*. Cambridge, Mass.: Harvard University Press, 1967.

Dziewanowski, M.K. *Poland in the 20th Century*. New York: Columbia University Press, 1977.

Fejto, Francois. *Eastern Europe Since Stalin: A History of the People's Democracies*. New York: Praeger, 1971.

Halecki, O. *A History of Poland*. New York: Roy Publishers, 1956.

Kirk, Grayson, and Nils H. Wessell. *The Soviet Threat: Myths and Realities*. New York: Praeger, 1978.

Liston, Robert A. *The United States and the Soviet Union*. New York: *Parents' Magazine Press*, 1973.

Roos, Hans. *A History of Modern Poland*. New York: Alfred A. Knopf, 1966.

Ulam, Adam B. *Expansion and Coexistence: Soviet Foreign Policy 1917–73*. New York: Praeger, 1974.

U.S. Congress, Senate Committee on Foreign Relations. *Perceptions: Relations Between the United States and the Soviet Union*, 1979.

Woods, William. *Poland: Eagle in the East*. New York: Hill & Wang, 1968.

Magazines and newspapers: *Foreign Affairs, Current History, The New York Times, Foreign Policy.*

INDEX

943
WO   Worth, Richard
        Poland

943   Worth, Richard
WO
        Poland

DATE	BORROWER'S NAME	